Dave loves all things trade! Dave's real passion is working with and learning from a vast variety of people in the trade industry. Dave held positions in government offices working as a Housing Officer and an Apprenticeship Trades Consultant. He thrives when he can help others excel in their chosen trade as he knows what it takes to be successful. Dave created the 7-step plan to guide anyone wanting to build a career as a certified journeyperson.

SPONSORS...

David E. Pocock

You're Hired and Certified

A 7 Step Guide to Apprenticeship in the Skilled Trades

AUSTIN MACAULEY PUBLISHERS®

LONDON * CAMBRIDGE * NEW YORK * SHARJAH

Ordering Information

Quantity sales: Special discounts are available on quantity purchases by corporations, associations, and others. For details, contact the publisher at the address below.

Publisher's Cataloging-in-Publication data
Pocock, David E.
You're Hired and Certified

ISBN 9798891557796 (Paperback)
ISBN 9798891557802 (ePub e-book)

Library of Congress Control Number: 2024913291

www.austinmacauley.com/us

First Published 2024
Austin Macauley Publishers LLC
40 Wall Street, 33rd Floor, Suite 3302
New York, NY 10005
USA

mail-usa@austinmacauley.com
+1 (646) 5125767

20250107

This book is dedicated to all those seeking
a successful lifetime career in the Skilled Trades.

Table of Contents

Introduction

Our lives depend on tradespeople. Tradespeople are the builders of our society and the creators of the lifestyle we all enjoy today.

Tradespeople are vital and essential to the world economy and the rewards of being certified are numerous and plentiful. The skills and talents of tradespeople are seen every day in the homes we live in, the buildings we work in, the sports facilities we enjoy, the infrastructure we use daily, the food we enjoy and personal care services. This is just a small example of the far-reaching talent of a tradesperson's contribution to our culture and community.

You're Hired and Certified explains the trades, the process and opportunities of obtaining a Journeyperson Certificate in seven easy steps. It covers everything from selecting a trade, to gaining employment, managing the apprenticeship and advancing your career after certification. The steps, practical lists and action exercises make this book a useful tool for anyone at all interested in learning more about the trade industry.

Apprenticeship training, Apprenticeship contracts and Certification can vary depending on location, industry and governments. Information in *You're Hired and Certified* has been written to support all trades and stakeholders dealing with the employment, training and Certification of Tradespeople.

Congratulations on taking the first step to achieving a successful lifetime career in the trades.

Who Should Read this Book?

For those who have reached this point in the book, this book is for you!

Determining a career path can be a somewhat daunting and confusing experience.

Perhaps you are a student or someone looking to change jobs and is considering a trade as a valuable and rewarding career option. Perhaps you are a career advisor such as a teacher or family member and are assisting someone needing to learn more about the trade industry. Perhaps you are an employer that recognizes the importance of training and development of employees. Or perhaps, you're a new apprentice and want to learn more about managing your apprenticeship.

Trades offer great careers and they also become steppingstones for advancement when additional education, work experience and confidence are gained.

This book will help all of you move forward by applying one or more of the seven steps to a successful career in the skilled trades. Also referred to as "The Apprenticeship Success Achievement Plan."

Part 1
Let's Talk Apprenticeship and Trade

What is an Apprenticeship?

An apprenticeship is an education program that is a combination of on-the-job training provided by an employer and the applicable technical training specific to the trade.

The training provided on the job is gained by working with someone who is already certified in the trade, is qualified by experience or is nearing the completion of the Apprenticeship Program such as a fourth-year apprentice training a first-year apprentice. A government or an industry organization typically provides the technical training.

Where are Apprenticeships Offered?

Apprenticeships are offered in most countries around the world. Trades offered will vary in different areas based on the need determined by governments and industry.

Training institutions will develop course material based on the determined need and administer the trade programs accordingly. These institutions work closely with governments and industries to manage Apprenticeship training and certification and all of the associated tasks.

The formal classroom-training component of an Apprenticeship program is typically offered in high-demand locations, such as regions where those industries exist or cities where there is a training institute or provider offering the program.

Our world is ever-changing, as is the demand for various trades.

What is a Trade?

Trades are occupations that offer a Certificate following completion of an Apprenticeship program involving technical training, on-the-job work experience and examinations.

Trades are designated a trade status by governments and industry associations where the need for skilled tradespeople is supported by industries in the area. As such, they are usually regulated by legislation or governed by a standards organization.

What are Trade Classifications?

A trade or trade work may be classified as compulsory or restricted, which means certification is necessary to perform tasks in the trade. Some examples are:

- Structural safety work
- Mechanical safety work
- Fire risk safety
- Gas safety
- Other public health or safety work determined by industry
- Professional standards established by industry

Public safety is one reason some trade activities may be restricted to individuals who have proven to be qualified to perform the tasks.

Trades could be classified as 'optional certification', allowing work to be performed without any mandatory requirements of a certificate. However, safety regulations may exist regardless of the classification of the trade.

What Industries are Trades in?

There is such a wide range of industries requiring trades, which makes it such an exciting career choice. Tradespeople work in a vast array of work environments in almost every sector of our economy.

Tradespeople are also involved in many business areas from management, to entrepreneurship opportunities as well as members in executive positions.

Trade School or University?

There are advantages for career advancement from the pursuit and completion of either a trade certificate or university degree.

The choice is really yours and they both can offer successful and achievable careers. It's all about what is right for you.

A trade certificate can be achieved for far less cost than a university degree as the apprentice is often paid while in training. Tuition fees are much less and are often covered by employers and some unions and associations provide tuition reimbursement. Government grants, scholarships and bursaries also often exist for apprentices.

A trade certificate is like a university degree in many ways. It is the stepping-stone, which often leads to advancing within a company and into other careers.

It's important to recognize that a trade certificate is a valuable accreditation much like obtaining a university degree with the difference being that the tradesperson has developed specific skills. Many of these learned skills transfer from one trade into other trade areas, which is another reason why tradespeople develop many other talents.

In addition to the technical skills learned, very important people and business skills are also inherent in the apprenticeship experience. These skills give a person the foundation and the confidence needed to move into many of the career paths that follow. It's proven, because I've witnessed it, that people who hold trade certificates have a strong commitment to success and are highly sought after by other employers in other industries. Trades provide skills and experience, which may lead to advancement within a company, into positions such as sales, estimating, contracting, supervision and management.

Trade and Journeyperson Certificate Benefits

Numerous benefits from wages to career advancement are attainable with a trade certificate.

Wages: You are being paid a wage while working and learning on the job and typically you will make more than many nontrade occupations. Your pay will increase as you advance through your Apprenticeship.

Confidence: You will gain valuable knowledge and experience allowing you to be a professional and expert in your field. You'll be proud and full of confidence.

Recognition and Accomplishment: You will be trade certified, a recognized credential for your accomplishment.

Portability: You carry your trade knowledge and skills wherever you live.

Career Advancement Opportunities: Many employment and career opportunities open up for holders of trade certificates.

The Apprenticeship Contract

Entering into an Apprenticeship contract involves a commitment on the part of the Apprentice as well as the Employer. Employers and the apprentice form the contract. You may also hear the term Sponsor which could refer to the employer, a Union or an Association.

An Employer could be a large corporation or in the case of Sole Proprietorship, the employer could be a one person, business owner. In either case, the parties would enter into a contract to support training on the job and any formal training leading towards the goal of the Apprentice becoming a Certified Journeyperson.

For the purpose of this book, we will use the term Employer, as that is typically the case for Apprenticeship contracts.

50 Common Trades

Many building, mechanical, service, industrial and specialized trades exist in every city or town. Trades will differ from region to region, based on how they are established, their demand and the industries that exist. Some examples are construction, manufacturing, fisheries, farming, mining and energy.

Here is a list of over 50 common trades; however, there may be many more in your area.

Building Trades: Carpenter, Electrician, Plumber, Refrigeration and Air Conditioning Technician, Roofer, Bricklayer, Cabinetmaker, Gasfitter, Sheet Metal Worker, Glazier, Lather (steel frame and drywall installer), Tilesetter, Painter, Concrete Finisher, Ironworker, Crane (Hoisting) Operator, Floorcovering Installer.

Mechanical Trades: Automotive Service Technician, Heavy Equipment Technician, Truck and Transport Mechanic, Auto Body Technician, Motorcycle Technician, Recreational Vehicle Technician, Agricultural Equipment Technician.

Service Trades: Cook, Baker, Hairstylist, Barber, Parts Technician, Landscape Gardener, Locksmith, Appliance Service Technician.

Industrial Trades: Millwright, Machinist, Welder, Boilermaker, Instrumentation Technician, Metal Fabricator, Insulator, Steamfitter/Pipefitter.

Specialized Trades: Powerline Technician, Power System Technician, Sprinkler System Installer, Elevator Constructor, Communications Technician, Transport Refrigeration Technician, Water Well Driller, Natural Gas Compression Technician, Outdoor Power Equipment Technician, Electrical Motor System Technician, Water Well Driller.

Advancing Within a Trade

As tradespeople advance in their careers, many will become managers, business owners, consultants, business partners and leaders in their area of expertise.

Entrepreneurship flourishes in many trades. Tradespeople gain experience and confidence leading those with ambition to the prospect of running their own business and hiring other tradespeople.

Key Messages

Apprenticeship programs are commonly regulated and administered by governments but some industries offer their own programs. These may be managed with government involvement or independently.

The demand for trades vary as do the Apprenticeship training programs and their locations.

The benefits of gaining certification in a trade are numerous, as are your choices in selecting a trade.

Action Exercises

1. Find available Apprenticeship programs in your area via internet searches.
2. Review the Apprenticeships offered to become more familiar with the trade options available to you.

Part 2
Apprenticeship Success
Achievement Plan

What is it?

The Apprenticeship Success Achievement Plan (ASAP) is a 7-step process that explains the why's and how's and the benefits of becoming a certified tradesperson.

ASAP usually refers to "as soon as possible" and is an appropriate acronym for this section. The purpose of this Apprenticeship Success Achievement Plan is to help you become successful, by getting a job in a desired trade, as soon as possible.

Use the information in this book to gain employment in the trade of your choosing. Follow through by managing your Apprenticeship to obtain your Journeyperson Certificate. Continue to invest in your education and always be aware of opportunities for future advancement. You will become an expert in your trade and a mentor to others.

Apprenticeship: Apprenticeship is a program where an employer provides on-the-job supervision to an employee in a trade and the employee completes a prescribed program of instruction. Completion of the Apprenticeship program leads to the designation of a Certified Journeyperson. Apprenticeship programs can vary depending on many factors including the complexity of the trade, the size of the trade, the availability and location of formal classroom training and the demand by industry for skilled workers in a particular trade.

Success: Every person will have his or her own definition of success. Some define success with possessions and wealth while others define success with happiness and health. One definition is "the progressive realization of a worthwhile goal." In other words, as long as you are progressing and moving forward towards a worthwhile goal you are successful. Being an apprentice is a path to success because you are working towards a very worthwhile goal.

The goal is to become certified in a trade. It will guide you to working at a professional level and achieving the success that is important to you.

Achievement: Achieving or accomplishing a task is related to an Apprenticeship where you are learning while performing. The best way to learn is by doing because it embraces all our physical and mental senses. An Apprentice's understanding is enhanced with the addition of formal technical training that will enrich their knowledge to ensure all aspects of the trade are learned, as the employer may not be able to teach all the relevant and necessary skills. Being part of the Apprenticeship program supports constant achievement, which in turn creates a rewarding learning experience.

Plan: Use this book as your plan for guidance and motivation. It will give you some comfort knowing you have a plan to follow. Incorporate the parts of this plan that are appropriate and relevant to your Apprenticeship and your employer. A key to success is taking action. At the end of each step are key messages and action exercises for you to build on your knowledge and to put your plan and activities into practice.

The 7 Steps to a Successful Career in the Trades

The 7 Steps require you to complete activities and to make decisions before moving on to the next Step. They are already in sequence to provide you with a plan. Although it is recommended to follow the Steps, you may skip Steps depending on your situation. I always suggest that if you are going to skip a Step that you take a few minutes to read through it just in case there is some information that may be helpful going forward.

At the end of each Step are action exercises challenging you to take some measures towards achieving your goals. The 7 Steps summarize the key activities that define Apprenticeship success from beginning to end.

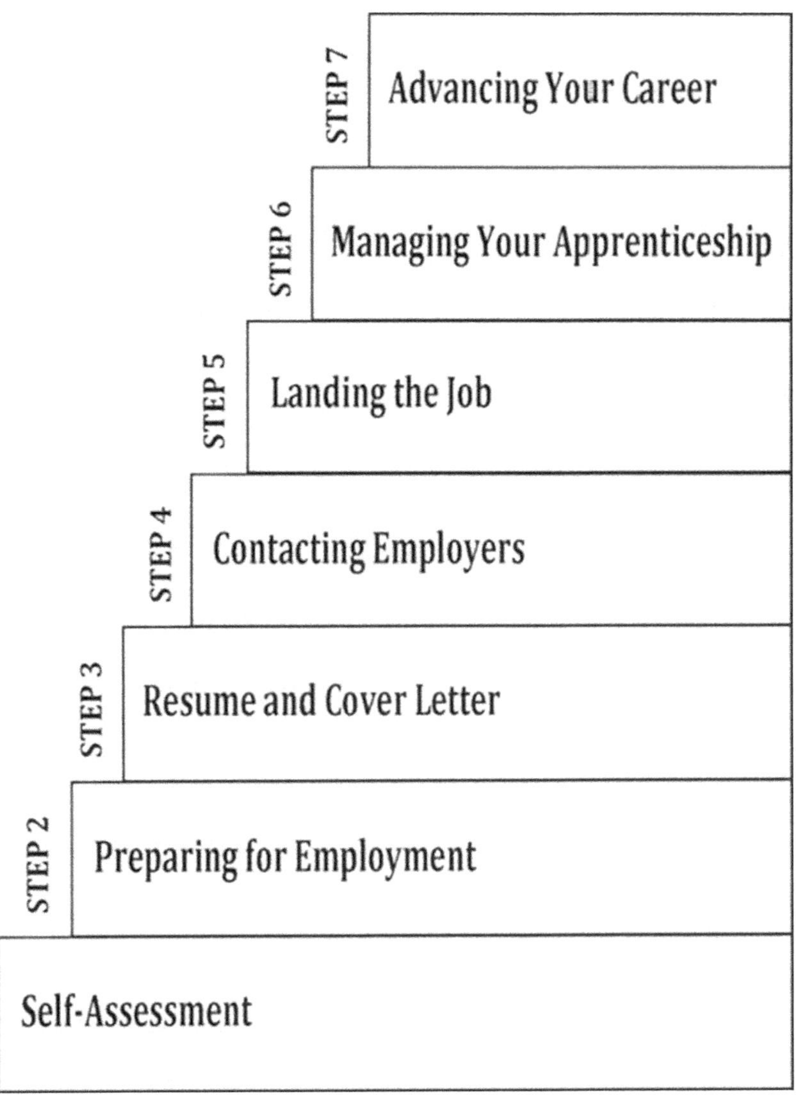

STEP 7
Advancing Your Career
STEP 6
Managing Your Apprenticeship
STEP 5
Landing the Job
STEP 4
Contacting Employers
STEP 3
Resume and Cover Letter
STEP 2
Preparing for Employment
Self-Assessment

Step 1
Self-Assessment

What is the Right Trade for Me?

The right trade for you is one you choose after you have completed a self-assessment considering personal criteria as well as the tasks associated with the particular trade.

Many people start working in a trade without giving the job any prior thought. A company was hiring and they needed a job so that's how they started. This may work for some people but it is not always the best approach. The best approach is to really think about what you would like to do and use that information to choose a trade that best fits with your goals.

Self-Assessment Questions

Answering some questions will help you determine the trades that you may consider pursuing and more importantly it will also identify those trades that you may not be well suited for.

The purpose of answering these questions is to harmonize your skills, interests and other factors such as financial, lifestyle, education level, physical strength and health.

Here is a list of questions to get you started. I would suggest that you have some quiet time to think about each question and how they apply to you. Examples of trades that may be applicable are provided for your consideration only; however, the list of potential trades is more numerous and ever changing.

The questions are numbered and you can write your responses in this book or document your responses in another manner for your review and analysis once completed. There may also be other aspects that are important to you that are not identified in this list, so I encourage you to consider those as part of the self-assessment.

1. What type of activity do you enjoy or is there something you have a strong interest or passion for?

Response:

2. Are you willing to work evenings, weekends, shift work or early mornings?

Response:

3. Do you have any work place health issues such allergies to dust and/or pollen?

Response:

4. Do you have a valid driver's license?

Response:

5. Can you work outdoors in winter and summer weather conditions?

Response:

6. Do you prefer to work with people or tools and machines or both?

Response:

7. Would you like to work with mechanical things like cars, trucks or machinery?

Response:

8. Are you artistic? Is it important to be creative in your work?

Response:

9. Are you interested in emerging technologies?

Response:

10. Do you like working with wood or building things out of wood?

Response:

11. Do you like working with various forms of metal?

Response:

12. Would you like to work in the residential construction industry?

Response:

13. Would you like to work on a large construction project?

Response:

14. Would you be willing to work at an industrial site that is located remotely?

Response:

15. Would you enjoy working in a manufacturing setting?

Response:

16. Are wages important in your choice of occupation?

Response:

17. Would you be willing to work in a confined space?

Response:

18. Would you work at high elevations?

Response:

19. Do you have physical limitations restricting you from manual labor?

Response:

20. Are you able to lift heavy objects such as a sheet of drywall, a sheet of plywood, a 50-pound bag of cement?

Response:

21. Are you interested in working with and helping people?

Response:

22. Are you interested in working in a farming or rural area?

Response:

23. Do you want to perform a variety of tasks?

Response:

24. Do you like working with plants, flowers, trees, lawns and landscapes?

Response:

25. Are you good at math, science and/or physics?

Response:

26. Are you able to perform calculations in both imperial and metric measurements?

Response:

27. Would you enjoy using various technologies and technology equipment?

Response:

Key Messages

Choosing a trade can be easy for some and difficult for others. Asking and answering questions can help get you started.

Internet searches allow you to learn more about the trades, which will help you select the right trade for you.

A self-assessment is the key to knowing what trade is right for you.

Action Exercises

1. Answer the self-assessment questions and list any other criteria that are important to you.

2. Complete internet searches for trades that are in your area or ones that you are interested in.

3. Identify the top three trades that interest you most considering your responses to the self-assessment questions and prioritize them in order of your preference using the Choice of Trade table below.

4. Understand the tasks, entrance requirements and timelines of the trades which may include the hours and months to complete.

Choice of Trade

Preferred Trade
Brief description
Entrance Requirements
Timelines:

Second Choice Trade
Brief description
Entrance requirements
Timelines:

Third Choice Trade
Brief description
Entrance Requirements
Timelines:

Step 2
Preparing for Employment

Goals

Now that you have selected a trade, it's important to write down your goals. People with goals succeed because they know what they want and where they are going.

Here is an example for you.

My goal is to become a Certified Journeyperson in the "Electrician" trade by "month and year."

Take a minute now to complete this line.

My goal is to become a Certified Journeyperson in the

_______________________________ **trade by** _______________________________

The next step is to support your goal with smaller goals and activities. One way to do this is to prepare a list of the activities required to meet your goal. It's important to know all the activities, what is required of each activity and the timing for each activity. At this time, you may not have a full activity list to complete your goal however, you can start your list and add to it as you move forward.

Here is a list for you to customize based on your goal.

Activity	Start Date	End Date
Research the trade of choice and the expectations of the job		
Determine entrance requirements and when they are required along with any education upgrading and/or safety training requirements		
Take stock of your finances		
Determine trade requirements (timelines, hours required, technical training, exams)		
Understand trade pay scale		
Identify any personal and/or safety equipment required including any specialized tools		
Review descriptions for each selected trade in detail		
Identify employment agencies and people that may help with potential employers such as friends and family		
Identify and build a list of potential employers		

Taking Stock of Your Finances

It is always a good practice to be knowledgeable of your financial situation to execute on your goals. You must know how much money is needed, when it is needed and your potential for making money during your Apprenticeship. At this time, understanding and being aware of resources available to you to assist with some of the costs is important as you move forward.

Pre-Employment Programs, Pre-Trades Training and Technology Programs

One strategy for getting a job in the trades is to attend formal training that positions you for employment. This is a course that an institute may offer which trains people to be ready and productive when they start an Apprenticeship. You can check the availability of programs with the local training institutes. They are often offered for major trades or where there is a demand from industry.

There are some advantages to pre-employment training for you to consider; however, this is just one option that may be available to you as an employment strategy depending on your chosen trade.

If this is an option for the trade you desire you may benefit in the following areas.

1. Completion of a pre-employment program shows the employer that you have made a commitment to the trade and want to be a Tradesperson. This is a real benefit for you and the employer.

2. Some employers will only hire those who have attended a course or program where the candidate to be hired has already received professional qualified instructions and practical school experience.

3. Some institutions can be instrumental in assisting students with potential employer networking opportunities and career counseling.

4. Some programs that you attend could provide part or all of your Apprenticeship training requirements.

Apprenticeship Program

Some trades may not have available pre-employment training and it also may not be what is right for you at this time. Going directly into the apprenticeship is a preferred choice for many so that skills can be acquired and money is being earned to support your Apprenticeship going forward.

If this is the desired option for your trade you may benefit in the following areas.

5. You will be earning an income as you learn on the job and you'll immediately be accumulating Apprenticeship hours.

6. The experience and knowledge gained will contribute to any formal training needed for Certification.

7. Your confidence and the satisfaction gained will keep you motivated and committed to your goal.

8. You immediately gain the real-life experience of the trade and learn from your mentor.

Apprenticeship Entrance Requirements

Some trades have no entrance requirements where others do. It's important to research and understand these requirements. Entrance requirements will differ, if they are applicable depending on complexity, knowledge level and the physical need of the trade.

If you do not meet the entrance requirements there may be a challenge exam option. Meeting these entrance requirements may not be a condition of starting the Apprenticeship but will at some point be required. As you move forward with your Apprenticeship, any entrance requirements will need to be planned for and the timing understood.

Create an Employer Contact List

When creating an employer contact list, it should be as extensive as possible to ensure you have every opportunity to gain employment.

Many jobs are never advertised to the public. People who have a connection to the employer may fill them. This is a good reason to network with family, friends, and everyone you know when you are looking for employment.

Some employers only accept applications through their website or use recruiters or their human resource staff to screen applications.

There are numerous avenues for you to prepare your employer contact list and you're encouraged to use every resource available to you including:

- Internet trade searches.
- Job search websites.
- Various media such as radio, TV, Instagram, Facebook and other social media applications covering News articles that may relate to employment opportunities.
- Career fairs.
- Recruitment and private employment agencies.

- Associations and Unions.

- Government sponsored/funded career training and employment agencies.

- Search relevant suppliers and ask if they know of any companies looking to hire.

- Networking with everyone you know including family, friends, previous employers and acquaintances.

- Job postings on employer storefronts and work sites.

- Libraries.

There may be a company that you have researched which you feel would be a good company to work for. If during your research it appears they are not hiring at this time, do put them on your list. Hiring conditions change all the time.

Key Messages

Preparing for employment is critical to finding employment. It is a necessary step that will only help increase your potential for success.

The employer list is your foundation moving forward. It is the key building block in achieving your goal. Your success depends on it.

Selecting a trade will require you to set your goals and make a plan.

Action Exercises

1. Share your goal with family and friends.
2. Customize the Employment Preparedness List based on your chosen trade.
3. Build your Employer Contact List. A sample and some blank lists have been provided for you. You will need much more but these will get you started.

Employer Contact List

Employer Name and Website	
Job details	e.g. First year Apprentice, location of job
Contact Information	e.g. Contact person name, email and phone number
Contact Date	e.g. Date contacted and method (to be added later)
Resume Sent	e.g. Date and method of sending resume (to be added later)
Follow up	e.g. To be added later
Results	

Employer Name and Website	
Job details	
Contact Information	
Contact Date	
Resume Sent	
Follow up	
Results	

Employer Name and Website	
Job details	
Contact Information	
Contact Date	
Resume Sent	
Follow up	
Results	

Employer Name and Website	
Job details	
Contact Information	
Contact Date	
Resume Sent	
Follow up	
Results	

Employer Name and Website	
Job details	
Contact Information	
Contact Date	
Resume Sent	
Follow up	
Results	

Employer Name and Website	
Job details	
Contact Information	
Contact Date	
Resume Sent	41
Follow up	
Results	

Employer Name and Website	
Job details	
Contact Information	
Contact Date	
Resume Sent	
Follow up	
Results	

Employer Name and Website	
Job details	
Contact Information	
Contact Date	
Resume Sent	
Follow up	
Results	

Employer Name and Website	
Job details	
Contact Information	
Contact Date	
Resume Sent	
Follow up	
Results	

Step 3
Resume

A resume is used to present yourself to potential employers and details your contact information along with your experience and skills.

It's important to express the trade you are interested in and to demonstrate your knowledge of the Apprenticeship program. By stating the trade you are applying for near the top of the resume you are telling the employer which trade you have chosen and your level of commitment.

This type of introduction is typically done at the top of the resume. Some employers may request a cover letter in addition to a resume. The cover letter content would include this detail.

There are numerous Internet sites that will guide you through preparing a Resume. You are encouraged to use what works best for you and for the job you are applying for. There may be some employment agencies that can offer assistance in your area.

Setting Up Email and Voicemail

Now is the time to review and/or set up an appropriate email and voicemail message. Employers need to contact you, which may include listening to your recorded voice message or sending you an email. These two contact options must sound and look professional. Avoid anything that could be interpreted as inappropriate.

Here's an example of a professional voicemail message that you may record. It's always best to record your voice mail message in an environment where there would be no background noise recorded.

"You have reached the voicemail of (Your Full Name). Sorry I missed your call. It is very important to me, so if you would be kind enough to leave a message, I will get back to you as soon as possible. Thank you."

For your email address, keep it simple using your name if possible. Ensure that your email address is friendly and not offensive.

Tips for Building a Resume

Here is a list of tips to use as a starting point in building your resume.

1. Write down all the skills and experience you have acquired so that you have a full inventory to choose from depending on the job opportunity.
2. Review sample resumes and determine what works best for you.
3. Use a format that is consistent and applicable for the job.
4. Use action words.
5. Add only relevant information.

Opening Statement

It is important that you state what your trade goal is so that the potential employer is clear on the Apprenticeship program, as it is not only your commitment but also, it's the commitment of an employer.

Here are some opening statement examples:

Example 1:

My goal is to Apprentice in the (Trade), working and training with a qualified person and improving my value by advancing in my trade to become a Certified Journeyperson.

Example 2:

My ambition is to Apprentice with a

(_____________________ Trade) company, improving my value while advancing in the Trade, aspiring to become a Certified Journeyperson.

Skills and Experience

Your resume will link your skills and experience to the competencies the employer has identified.

For those who have worked in a trade and have experiences to be included on a resume, use action words to describe them. Adjectives describe an attribute and are perfect to start short sentences on your resume under the skills and experience sections.

If you have no experience then you need to be a little creative by adding a couple of points to capture the attention of an employer.

Skills and experience can be realized in many ways and it's important to really think about what you have experiences in.

Consider other areas that are not specifically job functions such as hobbies and sports that may be relevant. For example, if you like to cycle and you fix your bike along with your family and friends' bikes, you clearly have mechanical and problem-solving skills. Another example is if you are an avid climber and enjoy this in your spare time, you are a great planner as you need to be prepared, you work well as a team member and safety is always a priority. This example could apply to many sports that you may participate in.

If you feel that you do not have any relevant experience it's important to think through things that you have done that are relevant to the job opportunity. Here are some ideas that may trigger mentioning on a resume in point form:

1. A reason for choosing this trade.
2. A relevant task you completed.
3. An experience working with people or teamwork.
4. An example of working with your hands.
5. A time you repaired or maintained something.
6. A related course or other career preparation training (high school, safety, first aid, etc.).
7. A related hobby or interest.

Key Action Words for Creating Your Resume

Demonstrated

Performed

Participated in

Delivered or Administered

Enhanced knowledge

Awareness of

Practical experience in

Experience dealing with

Developed practical skills

Trained in

Consulted with

Strong communication skills

Current member of

Worked with

Broad-based exposure to

Hands-on experience with

Managed or Supervised Troubleshooting with Assembled

Completed work orders for

Constructed

Fabricated

Education

The education portion of your resume will detail what school(s) you have graduated from, degrees that you have attained and/or any other forms of education you have completed or are in the process of completing.

This is also the section to identify any relevant awards or acknowledgements you have received.

If you already meet the trade entrance requirements it is important that you state this fact and place it at the beginning of this section so potential employers see this right away.

Here are some examples to get you started.

1. ____ Met the
entrance requirements for the _____________________

trade having completed Grade _____.

2._____________Completion of a career-planning program selecting
the _____________________ trade as my career choice.

3. _______________________________________ A proven interest in the
_____________ trade having completed a course in _____________________.

4. _____________________ Attended _________training to prepare for
working in the trade.

Volunteering and Hobbies

An additional heading which can be added to your resume is "Volunteering
and Hobbies." You can add this heading when these extra skills exist and
they indicate a relevant benefit to the employer.

Here are some examples:

- Adding hockey would be relevant if you play it and you are
  aware that other people employed in the company also play or
  support hockey or the position involves teamwork. This would
  apply for any team sport.

- Working on cars or bikes would be okay to add under hobbies if
  you were applying for a job in any of the mechanical trades.

- If you volunteered for Habitat for Humanity building homes and
  you are applying for one of the building trades then show this on
  your resume.

Volunteering can be a very rewarding and insightful experience. If you are
interested as an example in a specific home building trade, volunteering for
an organization such as Habitat for Humanity will provide you with firsthand
experience and knowledge. This will assist you in confirming if this is the
right trade for you and will also offer many industry contacts and hopefully
friendships along your career path.

Resume Scanning Software

Some employers, hiring managers and recruiters use a process of computerized resume scanning to sort through resumes. The scanning software identifies key words related to the job competencies. This technology saves the employer many hours of reading through hundreds of resumes. To ensure your resume gets the attention of the employer, be sure to address all competencies that are stated in the job description.

Key Messages

Your resume (and cover letter if required) is your entry point to potential employers. This is a critical and important step detailing your goals, skills, experiences and education.

Preparing your resume takes time but it's an essential step in moving forward with employment!

Action Exercises

1. Set up your email and voicemail if needed.
2. Use the Resume Building Table to get started.
3. Build your resume.

Resume Building Table

Your name and contact information
Introduction
Relevant skills and experience
Education
Volunteering and hobbies
Other

Step 4
Contacting Employers

Now that you have your employer list from Step 2 and your resume from Step 3 you are ready to begin contacting employers.

Congratulations on getting this far.

Record Keeping

It's very important to document all of your contacts and the status of those that you either plan to contact or already have contacted. A dedicated book either physically or electronically is required to ensure your record keeping is easily available and up to date.

You can use the Employer List Table that you created in Step 2 and supplement any further information required to help you manage this process going forward.

At a minimum, continuing from the Employer List Table in Step 2, here is the information you would want to record.

Company Name:

Contact Person:

Contact Email and Phone number:

Date Contacted:

Resume Sent:

Follow up actions:

Results:

Documenting this information is crucial for follow up. The data is valuable and important for networking and gaining employment. It also may be extremely beneficial in the event you are looking for work at a later time or you just want to change employers.

As you start the process of contacting potential employers, you may receive responses indicating they are not hiring at this time or you may receive no response at all. It's important to document this acknowledgement or lack of acknowledgment in the results section and set a time to check back. Some companies may be waiting to obtain approval for a contract or project and will be hiring once that approval is received. Always keep your eyes and ears open.

Customization is Important

It's important to ensure that your cover letter and resume address the specific requirements of the job you are applying for so it may be necessary to customize both of these documents. In order to keep track of which cover letter and resume you have submitted, it is recommended that you save the file with a meaningful file name such as the company name so you can access it quickly and easily.

Submitting Your Resume and Cover Letter

Typically, the first method of reaching out to potential employers is by submitting your resume and cover letter on their website. Some companies may have specific instructions on how to upload your resume or they may have a specific format where you would copy and paste your resume content in a predefined manner. Remember to always keep a record for every resume submitted.

Not all companies have websites and some may post a help wanted sign on their property or place a hiring ad in other various locations. In these instances, you will want to always have hard copies of your cover letter and resume with you. This can make the difference of getting the job or not. You never know when you may see an ad for a job position.

Tipping the Scale in Your Favor

The more resumes you send out the better chance you have of landing a job. It really is a numbers strategy at this point. If you only send out 2 resumes for example versus sending out 100 resumes, the likelihood of gaining employment is higher.

Sending resumes, talking to anyone and everyone about your goals and desired trade and staying focused will eventually lead you on your path to fulfilling your goal.

There are a number of methods to help you tip the scales in your favor in addition to sending lots and lots of resumes. You can pick up the phone and call companies that you are interested in, you can physically go to companies, you can continue searching out companies and you can again reinforce your goal and need for a job with family and friends. These tactics will definitely help you tip the scales in your favor.

Following up by Calling

One method of tipping the scale in your favor is by placing a phone call to the potential employer. If you are willing to do something that many others won't do, the results may put you right at the very top of their hiring list for a job interview.

Calling can be a very powerful tool. It shows initiative, demonstrates your communication skills and your commitment to the company and the trade you have chosen.

Think of placing the phone call as a mini-interview so you always want to make a great impression.

When you do call it's important to be in a quiet area with no background noise. Have your script prepared and practiced and have a pen and paper for note taking. You must also have your resume handy so if you are asked any questions you are ready to go.

I'm going to give you a sample phone script. It addresses the purpose of your call and is simple to use. Practice this script, get comfortable with it and modify it if you feel you need to.

Here we go with your script.

When you call a company, a front office individual will likely be the first to answer your call.

Hello, can I please speak with whomever is in charge of hiring the "Trade Name"?

If you are provided with the person's name, write it down immediately so you don't forget it and you can address the person by name if the call is answered.

When you are connected with the hiring person they typically answer with a greeting and their name. If not, that is okay, as you will follow through with your introduction and the reason for your call.

Hello "name of person if known," my name is…

The reason for my call is I am interested in the "Trade" and am hoping your company would consider me as a first year Apprentice. I meet the entrance requirements and am eager to start working.

You will likely receive an acknowledgement that "yes" the company is looking to hire first year Apprentices or "no" the company is not. Below are suggested responses to continue with the company's response.

Yes: Acknowledgement that the company is hiring at this time

Your response may be: ***"This is great news. I have my resume prepared and would be willing to drop it off for your review or send it to you by email."***

How the conversation continues may take many different paths. The main purpose of your conversation is to engage the hiring person in a manner that builds rapport and creates an opportunity to have your resume at the top of the list. Here are some tactics for you to consider depending on the conversation.

1. Offer to drop off your resume in person. If they advise you to send it by email to their general website, acknowledge that you have done that along with the date it was sent. You can also now offer to send it directly to the person you are speaking with.

2. Offer that you are willing to meet face-to-face for any interview opportunities.

3. Be prepared to answer why you want to work for this company.

When it is clear the conversation is ending always close with a message of being polite and thankful. Here is an example for you.

"Person's name," Thank you for taking the time to speak with me today. I really appreciate the discussion and I

- ***"will send my resume as discussed."***
- ***"look forward to meeting you."***
- ***"look forward to an interview."***
- ***"look forward to hearing back from you."***

No: Acknowledgement that the company is not hiring at this time

If the company is not hiring, you acknowledge the response and thank the individual for their time.

It is also good to indicate that you are still interested so if they were hiring at some time in the future you certainly would appreciate being considered.

This approach ends the conversation on a very good note and will be remembered if a job opportunity presents itself at a later date.

The companies that are not hiring are not rejecting you if they say no. They simply do not need to hire someone at this point in time. They may need someone at a later date and that is why it's important to document the conversation as part of your record keeping.

What if you get Voicemail?

Voicemail is something we are all used to receiving when we are calling someone. It is still an opportunity to reach out and leave a message.

When leaving a voice message, it is important to speak slowly and clearly. Practice the message below and time yourself to ensure it is no longer than 30 seconds.

Take a breath and at the sound of the beep be ready with your pre-scripted message. Your message is the same as if you did reach a live individual with the addition of your name and how they can reach you.

Hello __"name of person if known," my name is ____________________ .
The reason for the call is I am interested in the __"Trade Name"__ and am hoping your company would consider me as a first-year apprentice as I already meet the entrance requirements and am eager to start working.
I can be reached at __"Your phone number"__ and I look forward to hearing back from you. I hope you enjoy your day.

If you do reach voicemail, ensure to document this in your record keeping file along with a follow up date. If you follow up in a week and receive voicemail again, you could again leave another voicemail but this time it would be a slightly different message such as:

Hello "name of person if known," my name is ____________________ .
I called last week hoping your company would consider me as a first-year apprentice. I am still very interested and I can be reached at __"Your phone number."__ I look forward to hearing back from you and I wish you a good day.

If there's still no response after the second voicemail, it may be wise to ensure your resume has been submitted and leave it at that so you can focus on other potential employers.

The Physical Encounter

There are some companies that look for help by posting signs at their place of business or they advertise by other means such as Facebook, Instagram or a Newspaper ad.

Depending on your chosen trade, there may be industrial areas in your area, union offices and businesses that are looking to hire trades. Going to these areas prepared with your cover letter and resume is another opportunity to find Apprenticeship employment. This tactic offers a unique opportunity, as a potential employer will be able to meet you face-to-face so it's important to present a positive impression.

Again, it is like a pre-interview encounter that needs to be planned and prepared for. To ensure your resume looks clean and crisp, you can place your resume in a plastic sheet protector to ensure there are no wrinkles.

Practice your introductory message and, again, take a few deep breaths and relax beforehand.

Here is a sample introductory message.

Hello "name of person if known," my name is. I am interested in the "Trade Name" and noticed your ad for help wanted. I am hoping your company would consider me as a first year Apprentice as I already meet the entrance requirements and am eager to start working. Here is a copy of my resume and if there is someone I could speak to about the job opportunity that would be much appreciated."

Meeting a potential employer face-to-face is very powerful and shows that extra drive, commitment and initiative that employers are looking for. Your probability for success greatly increases when you are able to meet face-to-face. Some trades may not have the ability to implement this tactic but if the opportunity does present itself, it's a road worth taking.

Communicating, Communicating and more Communicating

Finding a job by word of mouth happens a lot. When starting out in the work force, resumes with skills and experience can at times look and sound very much the same. At the end of the day, skills can be learned; however, employers are looking to hire those individuals that demonstrate the "soft" skills that will carry them through the Apprenticeship. The more you continue to communicate with others, the more you are tipping the scales in your favor towards your Apprenticeship career.

Key Messages

To get the attention of a hiring resource, you can make phone calls or physically visit a potential employer to demonstrate your commitment and interest in becoming their employee.

Any opportunity for a face-to-face discussion with a potential employer is a key step to making a positive impression and increases your probability for employment.

Following up can really make a difference. It's this little extra that puts you ahead of the other applicants.

Keep communicating as networking can lead to employment.

Action Exercises

1. Keep reaching out to increase your probability of being hired.

2. Customizing your resume (and cover letter if required) to meet the needs of the potential employer is critical along with the necessary record keeping.

3. Ensure your employer list is updated and you have flagged the necessary follow-ups.

4. Document each follow up activity with key information such as date and whom you contacted.

Do something kind for yourself.

You've worked hard and have achieved a great deal.

Keep up the good work.

Step 5
Landing the Job

Preparing for an Interview

Making a good first impression absolutely increases your opportunity for a job offer so it's important to be prepared and confident.

There are numerous interview techniques used by companies and you really won't know which technique they use until you are being interviewed so it is best to be prepared. You can find lots of information on interview techniques and practice questions on the Internet and it is strongly recommended that you do some research and practice.

Many interviews are structured meaning they will ask all candidates the same questions so the hiring person is able to determine the best candidate(s). Behavioral-based questions are commonplace with questions focused around how you would deal with certain situations. An example might be "tell me about a time when you had a difficult situation and what tasks or actions you took and what was the result?"

Interviews for entry-level job opportunities tend to be more simplistic in nature versus applying for jobs requiring more experience and responsibility. It is always best to be as prepared as possible.

In addition to the interview questions, presenting yourself in a confident manner provides the hiring resource additional information about you that will be considered in the hiring process.

Below are some tips that you can consider and practice as you prepare for your interview.

1. Dress appropriately for the job interview.

2. Practice nonverbal communication such as eye contact, good posture, body language, facial expressions and tone of voice.

3. Fully understand your skills and what you bring to the company.

4. Listen carefully and try your best not to interrupt.

5. Your answer needs to respond to the question asked so you don't want to ramble on and on.

6. Use appropriate language.

7. Be positive and remain focused on your goal.

8. Be thankful and grateful.

Interviews can be completed in many forms now. Some interviews are face-to-face, some are done through video conference and some may just be a phone call. Interviews may also be completed on a one-on-one basis or with multiple people such as the hiring resource and a human resource individual. Regardless of the format, being prepared and bringing your best self to the table is all you need to do.

Interview Questions

Writing your responses to interview questions is a great way to prepare for your real interview. Below are some interview questions to get you started but you should add to these based on questions you may have found on the Internet, in discussions with family or friends or questions you may think they'll ask given your chosen trade.

1. How did you hear about this position?

Response:

2. Can you tell us more about yourself?

Response:

3. Why did you choose this trade?

Response:

4. Why should we hire you? (Explain why this trade is a good fit for you)

Response:

5. What is your goal/ambition?

Response:

6. Do you have any experience in this trade?

Response:

7. How do you handle a stressful situation?

Response:

8. Have you worked in a team environment?

Response:

9. What are your strengths and weaknesses?

Response:

10. How do feel about a steep learning curve?

Response:

11. Can you give an example of a challenge and how you handled it?

Response:

12. What computer skills do you have?

Response:

13. What's your biggest achievement?

Response:

14. Tell me about our company and our company values?

Response:

15. How would you handle a difficult person?

Response:

16. Do you have a valid driver's license?

Response:

17. Do you have your own vehicle or a reliable way to get to work?

Response:

18. When can you start?

Response:

The Mock Interview

A mock interview is an excellent way to practice and to get more comfortable with an actual interview. Interviews can be nerve racking but when you are well prepared they can actually have an element of enjoyment. Interviews form the foundation and basis for an employee and employer relationship. If the interview goes well, a decision to offer an employment opportunity is the next logical step forward.

You will want help with this exercise and it's best to find someone who has experience with interviews or someone you trust. Perhaps there is a friend or family member that can work with you. The person you choose will be able to offer you constructive feedback in an environment that is comfortable to you. If you're not able to find someone that can help you, this is also an exercise you can do on your own. It will feel a bit odd but trust your intuition and you'll know when you're feeling good about how you present yourself and how you respond to the interview questions.

Getting Prepared

In order to get ready for your mock interview:

- Select your mock interview questions and have them printed or available electronically for the interviewer.

- Bring a copy of your resume for the interviewer and for yourself along with something to take notes with.

- Ensure any electronic device you need has a full power supply.

- Try on the clothes that you plan on wearing to the interview to ensure they fit properly and you're comfortable in them.

Choose a room that provides a quiet setting similar to an office boardroom. Confirm the date and time for the mock interview.

Let's start the Mock Interview

The purpose of the mock interview is to help you improve your interview skills so you have the best opportunity to land the job. It's important to ensure the mock interview is as real as possible to gain the most benefit and learning.

When you meet the Interviewer, you will want to provide an introductory remark.

Introduction – "It's very nice to meet you (Add Interviewers name). Thank you for this opportunity. (Add your own opening remarks)"

The mock Interviewer will respond and you will both be seated across from one another at the table.

The Interviewer will typically start with some opening remarks and will begin asking the Interview questions.

You want your responses to sound natural and flow easily. Although you have written down your response to each question it's important that it does not sound like a memorized or mechanical response. This takes some practice and as your confidence builds so will your comfort level.

At the end of the interview questions, the Interviewer will typically close with a remark and may ask if you have any questions. You will want to consider how you respond to such a question, should this happen to you.

At the conclusion of the interview you will want to provide a closing remark.

<u>Closing – "Thank you for this interview opportunity. (Then add your own closing remarks)"</u>

The Mock Interview Feedback

This is the time when the Interviewer provides you with constructive feedback that will help you refine your interview skills going forward. It will focus on the overall impression you made, how your responses related to the questions being asked and any other areas that may have been a bit of a challenge.

Practice, practice and practice as much as you need to ensure you are confident and comfortable and ready for the real-life interview.

The Real Life Interview

You have planned and practiced and you are now ready for your interview. This is your opportunity to make a strong first impression and to demonstrate your skills, experience and commitment to your trade of choice.

A bit more planning is needed to ensure you experience the best possible interview so here are a few more tasks.

- Check the Internet to research the company and learn everything you can as you may be asked why you want to work for this company or to verbalize their corporate values. You can only respond based on what you have researched so it's important to dedicate some time for this task.

- Be clear on the requirements of your chosen trade (number of hours and years, entrance requirements, how to apply, technical training).

- Always get the Interviewers name(s) and their contact logistics.

- Be prepared to explain all of the content in your resume.

- Know where you are going and plan to be there at least 15 minutes early. A practice trip is always a good idea.

- It's also a good idea to have a few interview clothes chosen and ready to wear at a moment's notice.

Subcontract Work

Some companies may want to hire you on a subcontract basis as though you are working independently in your own business. This form of employment is not recommended for Apprentices.

If this is the only option, you should be aware of the disadvantages of not receiving certain benefits such as submitting taxes, employment insurance, workers compensation coverage, medical benefits and contributions towards pension that otherwise might be available. It may impact your ability to receive any financial assistance while attending formal training.

Working on a subcontract basis is typically for an experienced Certified Journeyperson who is already set up to run their own business.

Job Offers

After all your hard work and many interviews, a job offer will be received. Job offers can come in various forms, from a verbal offer immediately after the interview, to the waiting game that can span many days, weeks or even months. Since you contacted all the companies on your employer list, an offer would likely be greeted with great relief, excitement and a resounding yes!!!

If the offer is a written offer, ensure you read through it carefully. If you have any questions with respect to the offer, regardless of how it was received, do ask the hiring resource. Oh yes, and Congratulations!

You're Hired!

Key Messages

The Internet has no shortage of interview questions for you to consider. Mock interview exercises are the key to your interview success.

Being prepared by continuing to practice and refining your interview skills will ensure a good interview experience.

Action Exercises

1. Answer the example interview questions in this section and add others that you think may be applicable.

2. Complete as many mock interviews as needed and document the feedback items in the Mock Interview Feedback Form Table below.

3. Be prepared for your real-life interview by completing the Real-Life Interview Form. Research the company core values identified on their corporate website. It's important to know as much as possible so you are fully prepared for the interview.

Mock Interview Feedback Form

Example to completing the Mock Interview Feedback form

4. The response to interview question 6 regarding your experience with your previous employer did not come across in a strong manner.

Action: Use more action-oriented verbs and adjectives.

Status: Practice again during next mock session.

Mock Interview Feedback Form

<table>
<tr><td colspan="1">Date and Time
Location
Interviewer:</td></tr>
<tr><td>1.

Action:

Status:</td></tr>
<tr><td>2.

Action:

Status:</td></tr>
<tr><td>3.

Action:

Status:</td></tr>
<tr><td>4.

Action:

Status:</td></tr>
<tr><td>5.

Action:

Status:</td></tr>
</table>

6. Action: Status:
7. Action: Status:
8. Action: Status:

Real Life interview Form

Company Name: Date and Time: Location: Interviewer:

Company Website Link:

Summary of Company Details:

69

Company Name:

Date and Time:

Location:

Interviewer:

Company Website Link:

Summary of Company Details:

Step 6
Managing Your Apprenticeship

You are now hired so let's get you Certified!!!

Managing your Apprenticeship is essential to keeping your career moving in a forward direction. It is your responsibility to manage your Apprenticeship and it will entail many administrative and management tasks. Here are some of the tasks you get to look forward to and will need to do.

- Planning – looking ahead and setting objectives
- Being organized – keeping good records and properly recording hours worked
- Researching – seeking information on the formal training
- Communicating – discussions with employers and others
- Scheduling – attending training and examinations
- Coordinating – school expenditures, travel, residency, work
- Financing – arranging funds for technical training and making applications for any available support programs and loans
- Self-motivating – showing initiative by taking an active role and always maintaining a positive attitude
- Problem solving – overcoming any barriers and knowing that the steps to success involve overcoming any issues that you may encounter

Looking at this list of responsibilities it's plain to see why completing an Apprenticeship and obtaining Trade Certification is so valuable.

Your Apprenticeship Contract

An Apprenticeship contract forms an agreement between you and your employer unless determined otherwise by another authority.

The typical Apprenticeship contract should detail the things that need to be completed to gain Certification. Some Apprenticeship Trades may have just hours but many will show a requirement for both months and hours.

1. Hours and/or months to complete each period
2. Technical Training required
3. Examinations

Now that you are hired and your employer has agreed to the Apprenticeship contract, it is critical at this point that you are clear on what is required to manage your Apprenticeship going forward. You would have already done the research in a previous step but it's also important to check again to verify the Apprenticeship requirements.

Your First 30 Days

Here's a quick summary of some key points for planning after you gain employment and within your first 30 days on the job.

- Understand all of the Apprenticeship requirements and timing.
- Determine your employer contact for completing your Apprenticeship application.
- Focus on your new job, show up on time and do your best.
- Determine your plan for technical training school dates and schedules.
- Learn about any sources of funding that are available prior to attending training so you have sufficient resources.
- Make a tentative plan with your employer as to when you might attend the formal training.
- Keep track of the hours you work.

Apprenticeship Application

Getting registered as an apprentice is a very important task.

The apprenticeship application requires information from you and a portion also needs to be completed by the employer.

Employers may manage the Apprenticeship application at different times. Some will tend to it right away while others may want you to complete a probationary period, which is a period of time to ensure you are a good fit with their team. If the employer requires you to complete a probationary period first then you must ensure that you are not working on any tasks listed as compulsory until the application is approved.

It's critical that both you and the employer are clear on the activities you can work on to ensure compliance to the Apprenticeship requirements. Most employers are aware and will ensure that this is adhered to but it's also important for you to know and understand this as well for your own safety and for the safety of others.

One of the most important people in the organization for you to connect with is the individual or team that manages the Apprenticeship application. Ensure you have all of your information completed and schedule the necessary time with the individual responsible for Apprenticeships in the company.

On the application there may be a section dealing with any previous experience where you can show what companies you worked for as well as tasks performed and hours worked. This can be important if you want to receive any credit for any past experience. Gather all of your previous records and document this information on your application, if applicable. Receiving any additional credit along your path to Certification will expedite you to success that much faster.

Once the application has been submitted, keep a copy for your records and follow up, if required. Typically, you will receive a positive acknowledgement unless there is information missing on the application.

Meeting the Trade Entrance Requirements

Trades may have entrance requirements that vary depending on the technical difficulty of the trade. The entrance requirements are important to ensure you have the required basic knowledge to be successful in your Apprenticeship.

If you do not meet the minimum trade entrance requirements there may be an entrance exam alternative. It is your responsibility as an apprentice to investigate this information and submit transcripts and/or schedule yourself to take an entrance exam. This is necessary to become eligible to attend formal training. Remember, if you do an exam and do not pass, you'll need to upgrade your skills/training and take the exam again. If necessary, repeat the process until you are successful.

Treat failing any exam as an opportunity to better your knowledge in the areas where your mark was below the passing grade. Failure is one stepping stone to success.

The timeframes associated with passing the entrance requirements differ so this task must be planned for accordingly.

Attending Formal Training

Most of your Apprenticeship is learned on the job; however, the technical training teaches the technical areas of the trade and also reinforces correct procedures and methods.

An Apprenticeship is a training program which generally involves 80% on the job training and 20% of your time in formal training, regardless of the delivery method. Therefore, you are training while working and learning through the formal training to achieve a Journeyperson Certificate.

In order to get all the information needed to plan for your formal training, you will want to spend some time on the Apprenticeship and/or the training institute website to determine the where, what, when and how much.

The website will provide you with the following information.

- Where are the training locations?
- When does the training schedule come available for the year and when, where and how is the training offered?
- What are the fees for tuition and books?

Review with Your Employer

Based on the information you've researched; you will be in the best position to determine when attending the training would be best for both you and your employer. You will also know what financial resources or programs you may be eligible for.

With all of this knowledge you can now have a discussion with your employer to agree on the best timing for you to attend the training. Review your proposed training schedule together to determine which dates will work best for the company. This is also a good time to discuss any financial assistance offered by the employer.

Employers have agreed to the Apprenticeship contract so they do understand the need and value of formal training. If during the conversation you sense some hesitancy, you can always draw on these points to ensure the benefits of training are well understood.

- Productivity – training will help me boost my speed and production adding more value to the company
- Competency – training will increase my ability to accomplish my work successfully
- Quality – training will increase my level of excellence so that I'm providing a professional service to our clients
- Credibility – training will benefit the company by improving trust which is important for repeat business and referrals

Traveling to Attend Formal Training

Depending on where the formal training is located, you may need to travel to complete this portion of your Apprenticeship.

You will already know if this is applicable to you based on your previous research.

If the training location is beyond the normalcy of a daily commute you will need to make the necessary arrangements to temporarily relocate for the training period and will need to ensure your finances are in order to pay for temporary accommodations, travel, food, parking and any other expenses that will be incurred.

The Benefits of Formal Training

Sometimes it's important to remind yourself of all the reasons and benefits of
continuing on, especially if you are experiencing challenges related to the
job, your employer, co-workers, personal health, financial or family difficulties.
Recognize that everyone has challenges and overcoming them is what builds
good character and makes you a great Tradesperson.

Keep in mind the following benefits of completing the formal training:

- To advance one level in my Apprenticeship.
- To get a pay increase.
- To learn the correct methods and become an expert.
- To gain confidence in my work.
- To improve my self-esteem and job satisfaction.
- To be qualified to mentor/train other Apprentices.
- To improve my chances for a company promotion.
- To avoid loss of future income and career opportunities.
- To achieve my goal to become a Certified Journeyperson.

Financing Your Apprenticeship Training

Attending the formal classroom training means doing some financial
planning to ensure you have funds for the tuition fees, books, living costs and
travel, if required.

There are a number of financial support possibilities for you to pursue. It's to
your benefit to ask your employer and other agencies what financial options
are available to you so please do ask and apply for those that are relevant.
Here are some items for you to consider:

- Your savings.
- Family support.
- Employee savings/payroll deductions.
- Employer support for tuition fees, books or other costs.
- Union support for tuition fees.

- Trade association support for tuition fees.

- Employment Insurance for Apprentices.

- Loans from schools, governments, financial institutions.

- Scholarships and bursaries.

- Government support programs and grants.

Passing Exams

Exams can be stressful and you may experience some anxiety. This is all quite normal. One of the best ways to manage these feelings is to be well prepared.

To help you get prepared for the exam it is a good idea to take plenty of notes during class, ask questions if you are unsure of something and studying with a partner is a great way to reinforce the content learned in class.

You may want to consider using flash cards as a method of enhancing your memory recall. Use whatever method works for you. Committing to and setting aside a pre-determined time for studying will make a huge difference. A good practice is to take some time to review your notes after each class as this will reinforce the days learning and you'll be better prepared for the next day's training.

Find a study partner, someone to brainstorm with, as this will benefit you both in many ways. You will share and discuss the training material which will reinforce the learning and better prepare you both for the exam.

On exam day, take a deep breath and reassure yourself that you have done your best. Good luck, you've got this.

Stay Focused on Your Goal

There may be times when you find it challenging to stay focused on your goal and that is very normal. Stay the course and become a Certified Journeyperson.

Record, Review and Manage Your Apprenticeship Information

Your hours worked, months completed, training and exams are all items that need to be recorded with the Apprenticeship authority as they will be issuing you the Journeyperson Certificate. Getting this information submitted and documented to your file on a pre-determined scheduled basis is an important task.

The employer typically records the hours and months depending on the rules of the Apprenticeship program you are enrolled in. They are recorded as specified in your Apprenticeship contract. If employment ends, make sure your work hours are documented and recorded with the appropriate authority.

The schooling and exams are done during your Apprenticeship and should be automatically recorded unless you completed a pre-employment program or have accreditation from other training (high school or college program) or another related Apprenticeship.

Keeping all of your records in a safe place for you to refer to in the future may make a difference if there is ever a discrepancy that requires correction. Please do not throw out any material related to your employment such as pay stubs showing hours worked and education and training receipts. It may be needed at some point to prove the Apprenticeship requirements were met.

Review your contract details after you receive the documentation from your Apprenticeship authority. Check for any errors in your contract and if they exist discuss them with your employer. Contact the Apprenticeship authority and take the steps needed to amend any errors, omissions or discrepancies in your contract.

Keep up the Good Work and Be Safe

Your employer has a reputation of quality work which is vital for referrals and repeat business. It's important to learn the proper procedures and to do the very best work that you can.

As an Apprentice you are learning while working to become a Certified professional and an expert in your field. As you acquire the knowledge and skills by being mentored, you will become a more productive and valuable employee. This is one reason why Apprentices' wages increase after completing each period of their Apprenticeship.

In order to achieve the best learning experience here are some key points for you to consider.

- Stop and think about your work.

- Ask questions; never be embarrassed about asking a question.

- Seek expert advice and extra help when needed.

- Ask what is better, what is faster and what is more economical to better understand the task at hand.

- Learn the best sequence for getting the work done correctly.

- Always think about working safely and wearing the proper personal protection equipment when appropriate.

- Never do work when it's unsafe or you lack the competencies to perform the tasks safely and correctly.

Every trade requires you to think about the work you are doing so you and those around you are always safe. Never do something that has an element of danger until you have received instruction from your supervising Journeyperson or experienced trainer. Attend the safety courses and meetings and always ask if there is something you are not sure of. The health and safety of workers in all trades is something that requires constant awareness and continuous practice by every employee.

Keeping your Apprenticeship Active

Life circumstances may take you in a different direction, which could have an impact on your Apprenticeship. If you do find yourself in this position, it's important to reach out to the Apprenticeship Authority to determine your options to remain as an active apprentice.

Delayed or incomplete record keeping may also impact the status of your Apprenticeship. Being aware of your responsibilities in advance can help you avoid the cancellation of your Apprenticeship. Your Apprenticeship active status could be changed to a cancelled status if you are in any of the following situations.

- Not keeping your information current such as your contact and employer information.

- Not progressing or dormant after a period of time such as not advancing a level within a prescribed period of time.

- Not meeting the entrance requirements within a prescribed period of time.

- Not attending training or not completing exams within a prescribed period of time.

- Not having an active training contract with an employer such as leaving your employer to become self-employed or changing employers without notifying the Apprenticeship Authority and amending your training contract.

If your Apprenticeship does change to a cancelled status, you should contact the Apprenticeship Authority. There could be a small fee to be reinstated or you may need to complete a new application. If you do not want to continue with the completion of the Apprenticeship it is still a good idea to contact the Apprenticeship Authority and advise them of your decision.

You Got This – Your Path to Success

You are now prepared to complete your path to success and are clearly determined to make it real.

- You have a goal and are focused on achieving your goal.

- You understanding the Apprenticeship program, the expectations and your Apprenticeship contract.

- You are well informed; you ask questions or you've researched the required information.

- You demonstrate your passion and desire to be successful.

- You own and take the responsibility to manage your Apprenticeship by keeping track of your hours worked.

- You have set up your finances and have applied for all financial assistance available to you.

- You are executing your Apprenticeship contract as planned including working the hours and attending formal training and exams.

- You are always showing up for work with the can-do attitude and are eager to do and learn.

- You know the timing of the formal training or exams and have all the necessary logistics in place to attend along with the support from your employer.

You are always keeping your eyes on your goal.
Congratulations!!!

Celebrate

You have finished your final exam and you can now take a very deep breath. Now it's the waiting game to see if you have passed. Whoever is overseeing the exam process will advise you when and how you are notified of your exam results.

You may receive an email with the results or perhaps you will be advised to go to an online portal with your account information to see your results. Whatever the outcome is, the learning experience itself is a major accomplishment.

You have one more important step and that is to follow up with the Apprenticeship Authority to ensure all your requirements are accurately reflected and your Certificate is being processed as proof of completion.

You Are a Certified Journeyperson!!!

Key Messages

The Apprenticeship application and all the associated record keeping requirements are important steps in managing my Apprenticeship.

Managing your Apprenticeship is your responsibility. It will require you to plan, set goals and stay on track through to completion.

Action Exercises

1. Complete the Apprenticeship Management Chart
2. Complete the Managing My Apprenticeship Chart
3. Complete the Apprenticeship Training and Exam Financial Chart

Apprenticeship Management Chart

Apprenticeship Management Chart	
Hours to Complete Each Period	
Months to Complete	82
Technical Training Requirements	
Examination Dates and Times	

Managing My Apprenticeship Chart

Managing My Apprenticeship	
Employer and Supervisors Name and Number	
Start and End Dates	
Hours Worked	
Months Worked	
Tasks Performed	

Employer and Supervisors Name and Number	
Start and End Dates	
Hours Worked	
Months Worked	
Tasks Performed	

Managing My Apprenticeship	
Employer and Supervisors Name and Number	
Start and End Dates	
Hours Worked	83
Months Worked	
Tasks Performed	

Employer and Supervisors Name and Number	
Start and End Dates	
Hours Worked	
Months Worked	
Tasks Performed	

My Apprenticeship Training Financial Chart			
Activity	**Amount**	**Date Required**	**Source of Funds**
Tuition Fee			
Books			
Laptop (if required)			
Travel expenses			
Living costs			
Food			
Incidental expenses			
Existing monthly expenses			
Parking			
Work related clothing			

Step 7
Advancing Your Career

Invest in Yourself

Your Journeyperson Certificate proves you have achieved a level of competency in a trade. The job experience and Trade technical training has given you the skills and the working knowledge of the business activities and a confidence level of a professional Tradesperson. Now is a good time to consider additional training in areas that will enable you to advance within the company or into other careers.

Tradespeople who know the business from the operational level make excellent managers and business owners when they learn and gain experience in the relevant business areas.

Gaining this experience can come in many ways. Just as your Apprenticeship was structured, on-the-job training is a great way to gain other skill sets along with real work-life experiences. Another method is to attend courses offered by your employer or by other learning institutes like colleges and universities through their continuing education programs. Today there is a considerable number of courses that you can take online, enabling you to learn and study in your free time.

If advancing your career is something you are wanting and determined to do, you can follow similar steps you have taken to achieve your Certified Journeyperson Certificate. Set your goal and create your career path plan.

To prepare your plan, you will need to identify the skills and work experience required to make your plan successful. To get you started, below are some subject areas you may want to consider.

Subjects for Learning Business Competencies:

- Business Administration
- Finance, Budgeting
- Supervision
- Leadership
- Marketing and Sales
- Management
- Project Management
- Public Administration
- Accounting
- Business Law
- Business Mathematics
- Communications
- Economics
- Human Resource Management
- Industrial Labor Relations
- Information Technology/Computer Software Training

Industry Specific Training

If you really love your trade, another great option for advancing your career is to specialize in a very niche area of your current trade. Learning a specialty and becoming an expert in one or more areas can lead to a niche position of employment adding value to your trade and to your paycheck!

Many trades have advanced training or specialty courses that are outside the scope of the initial trade course outline. These courses may be offered by a college or institute or by an association, union, manufacturer or private training provider.

Values and Expectations

Whether you are working alone or in a team, your motivation, enthusiasm and hard work are key attributes companies look for in an employee. Many companies list their work values, which help to define their ethics, principles, attitudes and work expectations. You want to perform according to these expectations to stay employed and to be considered for advancement.

Some examples of values are:

- Quality
- Respect
- Honesty
- Integrity
- Teamwork
- Responsibility
- Accountability
- Continuous learning
- Diversity
- Leadership
- Innovation

Mentoring

Considering that an Apprenticeship involves on-the-job training by employees mentoring other new employees, it stands to reason that someday your turn may come when you are asked to mentor a new Apprentice. This process is how companies grow and how people move up within a company. Therefore, you may be required to train someone in your current role. When the time comes, be ready and willing to accept this as an opportunity to grow and learn new things. If you strive to raise the bar by being a better mentor, you will be adding tremendous value to both future Apprentices and to the company. Be the best mentor you can be and amazingly your influence will be passed on down the line.

Being a good mentor is an important responsibility!

As a mentor to a new Apprentice there are several topics for you to discuss. The following list will provide a good start to the mentoring relationship.

Apprentice and Employer Orientation Topics

1. When and how to do the application for Apprenticeship.
2. Review the trade requirements and prepare the Apprenticeship contract which generally includes hours and months of work required, technical training and examinations.
3. Review the apprentice and employer responsibilities in managing the Apprenticeship contract.
4. Discuss recording hours and managing records.
5. Review the technical training schedule for locations and dates.
6. Review the cost of tuition fees, books and other anticipated expenses.
7. Review what financial assistance may be available from all possible sources.
8. Discuss the importance of Certification and the benefits to both the apprentice and the company.
9. Discuss company policies on Apprenticeship with respect to challenging exams, scheduling school, attending training, keeping records, tuition fees and wages.

Key Messages

Always invest in yourself and career opportunities will open up for you.

When you further training, you become a better mentor and position yourself to move upward in your career.

Action Exercises

Keep this book to reference often, as a reminder of your success!!!